O. W. HOL   RY

DEMCO

DJUSD
Public Schoo
Library Protection A

D1123074

Your
Travel
Guide to

ANCIENT
MAYAN
CIVILIZATION

Your
Travel
Guide to
ANCIENT
MAYAN
CIVILIZATION

Nancy Day

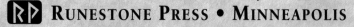

RUNESTONE PRESS • MINNEAPOLIS

A DIVISION OF LERNER PUBLISHING GROUP

Designed by: Zachary Marell and Tim Parlin
Edited by: Kari Cornell and Martha Kranes
Illustrated by: Tim Parlin
Photo Researched by: Glenn Marier

Runestone Press
A division of Lerner Publishing Group
241 First Avenue North
Minneapolis, Minnesota 55401 U.S.A.

Website address: www.lernerbooks.com

Library of Congress Cataloging-in-Publication Data

Day, Nancy.
    Your travel guide to ancient Mayan civilization / by Nancy Day.
      p. cm. — (Passport to history)
    Includes bibliographical references and index.
    Summary: Takes readers on a journey back in time in order to experience life during
the Mayan civilization, describing clothing, accommodations, foods, local customs,
transportation, a few notable personalities, and more.
      ISBN 0–8225–3077–5 (lib. bdg. : alk. paper)
    1. Maya—Juvenile literature. [1. Maya—Social life and customs. 2. Indians of
Mexico—Social life and customs. 3. Indians of Central America—Social life and
customs.] I. Title. II. Series: Day, Nancy. Passport to history.
F1435.D38   2001
972.81'016—dc21   99–38688

Manufactured in the United States of America
1 2 3 4 5 6 – JR – 06 05 04 03 02 01

CONTENTS

INTRODUCTION

GETTING STARTED

Welcome to Passport to History. You will be traveling through time and space to the ancient Mayan civilization of A.D. 600 to A.D. 800. This travel guide will answer such questions as:

- ➤ **Where should I stay?**
- ➤ **What do I wear?**
- ➤ **Which local dishes should I try?**
- ➤ **Who should I meet during my visit?**

Remember you are going back in time to an ancient culture. Some of the things to which you are accustomed—such as electricity—didn't yet exist. So forget packing your video games, hair dryer, medicines, watches, and other modern conveniences that would make your stay a lot more comfortable. Don't even bother to bring a camera. Cameras didn't exist during the ancient Mayan civilization, so all of the pictures in this book are either drawings or photographs made after the invention of photography. But don't worry. The locals do just fine without all of these gadgets, and with a little help from this book, you will too.

Modern-day visitors to the Mayan ruins at Chichén Itzá investigate the Temple of Kukulcan. The ancient Mayan civilization of Mexico and Central America intrigues and mystifies modern tourists and scientists.

NOTE TO THE TRAVELER

Use this guide as a resource for what to expect during your visit to the ancient Mayan civilization. Information about how the Maya lived comes from archaeologists, who examine the remains of Mayan buildings, tools, and artworks. Other information comes from ancient Mayan texts and documents left by Spanish explorers and settlers.

Some Native American peoples have an expression they use after telling a story. They may say, "That is how it was told to me." This is a way of acknowledging that there may be other versions, variations, or interpretations. Some of the information on Mayan culture came from

NORTH AMERICA

GULF OF MEXICO

Teotihuacán •

Chichén Itzá •

Palenque •

Tikal •

PACIFIC OCEAN

CENTRAL AMERICA

the Spanish, who encountered the Mayan people hundreds of years after the period you are visiting. The Spanish brought their own biases to their interpretations of Mayan ways. Mayan rituals seemed quite foreign to the Spanish. Their reports have, in some cases, been copied and translated several times, which makes them even less reliable.

Bishop Diego de Landa, one of the first Spaniards to meet the Maya, recorded a great deal of valuable information about the Mayan culture in the 1500s. But he also destroyed many important original Mayan documents and artifacts. The Christian Spaniards burned Mayan texts because they felt that the documents contained beliefs that were not Christian. The bishop wrote, "We found a large number of books . . . and, as they contained nothing in which there were not to be seen superstition and lies of the devil, we burned them all. . . ."

Of the few Mayan texts that survived, many have been lost through neglect or deterioration. Fortunately, some information was also carved into stone monuments, buildings, and artifacts that still exist. However,

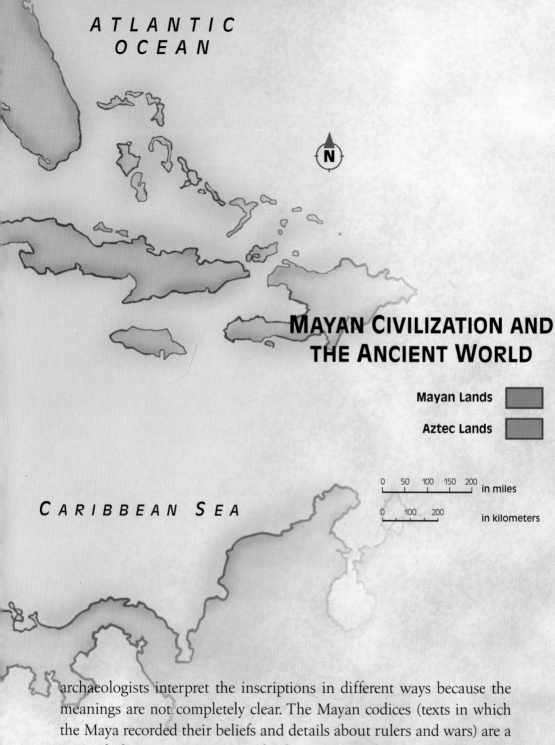

ATLANTIC
OCEAN

CARIBBEAN SEA

MAYAN CIVILIZATION AND THE ANCIENT WORLD

Mayan Lands

Aztec Lands

0	50	100	150	200	

in miles

0	100	200	

in kilometers

archaeologists interpret the inscriptions in different ways because the meanings are not completely clear. The Mayan codices (texts in which the Maya recorded their beliefs and details about rulers and wars) are a particularly important source of information. Unfortunately, only parts of four codices have survived. One of the most important is the Dresden Codex, a detailed, well-preserved document that helps archaeologists understand the ancient Maya. So although this book provides a good starting point for your visit to the ancient Mayan civilization, remember that you may find some things contradict what is described here.

The sun sets on Chichén Itzá. The ancient Mayans pay careful attention to astronomical events when building religious temples.

WHY VISIT THE ANCIENT MAYA?

The Mayan culture has existed for nearly four thousand years. At its peak, it was one of the most brilliant and powerful cultures in ancient America. The Maya built great cities, formulated a sophisticated calendar, and developed a complex belief system. The ancient Mayan civilization lasted from approximately 2000 B.C. to A.D. 1500. Historians call the period from A.D. 250 to A.D. 900 the Classic period. This was a time of growth, when the population and size of the settlements reached their peak. Within the Classic period, the ancient Mayan civilization was rejuvenated between A.D. 600 and A.D. 800, after a period of little or no growth.

By this time, the Maya had developed sophisticated mathematics and time measurement systems. They calculated the movements of the planets, determined the exact length of a year, and built observatories to study events in the sky. They built cities and developed a government. The Maya recorded their religious beliefs using an advanced writing system. They exchanged ideas and goods with other cultures through trade.

Beginning in about A.D. 800, the Maya abandoned many cities, which were soon taken over by flourishing plants. Historians aren't sure what led to this decline, but they do have theories. One guess is that disease wiped out much of the population, and those who survived chose to move elsewhere. Others believe that Mayan farmers may have over-worked the soil in these abandoned settlements. When they weren't able to locally grow the food they needed, the Maya moved to new areas. Or a major earthquake or hurricane may have destroyed the settlement, and the Maya chose to move rather than rebuild. Widespread warfare may have pushed inhabitants from their homes. Yet the Maya did not die off completely.

In the 1500s, Spanish explorers arrived. They brought new weapons, an entirely different culture, and they unknowingly introduced new diseases. They forced the Maya to work as slaves and claimed Mayan temples as treasures for the Spanish king. Even with these hardships, the Maya managed to survive. They fled to areas outside Spanish control or rebelled against the Spanish. They built new settlements, including a new capital at Chichén Itzá. In modern times, the Mayan people still practice many of their ancient beliefs and traditions.

Keep in mind that most of the original Mayan names for cities have been lost. The Spanish renamed some of the cities during the Spanish Conquest of the 1500s. Historians and archaeologists sometimes re-named the ruins of abandoned cities as they discovered them. To avoid confusion, this book will refer to the names that are used in modern times, unless otherwise noted.

THE BASICS

LOCATION LOWDOWN

In the Classic period, the ancient Mayan civilization is located in an area of what will one day be southeastern Mexico, Guatemala, Belize, El Salvador, and Honduras. About the size of New Mexico, the territory of the ancient Mayan civilization covers one of the most diverse regions on Earth. Most of the area rests on the Yucatán Peninsula, a portion of land that juts out into a body of water. To the north and west of the Yucatán lies the Gulf of Mexico. The Caribbean Sea washes the peninsula's eastern shore.

In the north, you will find dry lowlands covered with stunted trees and scrub. This area is home to the Mayan centers of Chichén Itzá and

Dense rain forest shrouds the remains of an ancient Mayan structure at Palenque.

Uxmal. As you travel farther south to the central part of the Mayan region, you will pass into areas with greater rainfall, where lush rain forests thrive. The Mayan centers of Palenque and Tikal are found between the tangle of trees.

The rain forests are home to a wide variety of plants and animals. Avocado trees provide food. Vanilla vines and allspice trees yield seasoning for food. Trees such as mahogany, cedar, and palm provide wood or thatch for building. Ramón trees grow everywhere. Because ramón nuts can be stored for long periods, the Maya keep them for times of famine (food shortage). Parrots, toucans, woodpeckers, doves, and many other birds fill the trees. Dragonflies and butterflies, including the famous blue morpho, flutter through the air. You may see anteaters, ocelots, jaguars, and many other animals that the locals hunt for food, including deer, tapirs, and rabbits. Rivers flow through the southern lowlands and empty into the Caribbean Sea. On the lowland coast, the sea brims with shrimp, spiny lobsters, crabs, manatees, and sea turtles. In these areas, shellfish are the main source of food.

13

IMPORTANT
Safety Tip

Don't be tempted to hunt the quetzal for its exquisite feathers. The locals respect this bird so much that killing one without permission can be punishable by death.

As you work your way even farther south, you will find highlands. Steep slopes make some areas impossible to farm. Many of the Mayan settlements are located in valleys between the mountains and hills, where crops grow well and water is plentiful. A beautiful tropical bird called the quetzal lives in the highland rain forests. You may also see howler and spider monkeys, weasels, foxes, armadillos, parrots, coatimundis, and kinkajous.

The highlands also contain deposits of rocks and minerals, especially jade, which the locals value highly. Earthquakes often strike, and volcanoes erupt in the highlands, too.

CLIMATE

The climate here changes depending on where you are. Lowland areas close to the sea are much hotter than mountain regions. You will be warmer in the northern lowlands, where the temperature averages 86°F, than in the mountainous areas to the south, where the temperature averages only 63°F.

If you travel to the southern highlands during the summer, you should be aware that the rainy season lasts from May to December. The days often start out clear. But late in the day, clouds bring rain and sometimes thunderstorms. The storms tend to be hit or miss, however. If you ask the locals whether it will rain on a particular day, they may simply respond, "It might." In the rain forest, you can count on sticky, humid weather. You'll want to air out your clothes in the sun, otherwise they will become green with mold.

Winters are quite dry. Drought can be a problem. Long periods with no rain can kill crops and cause food shortages. So the locals have come up with some creative ways for catching and preserving water. You may see reservoirs, underground pits for storing water, and sophisticated drainage structures for carrying excess water to crops.

Hot Hint

Watch for the Uo frog. The locals know that when the Uo frog comes up from its underground home, the rainy season is about to begin.

LOCAL TIME

Although you may feel naked without your watch, you will find that the Maya are excellent timekeepers. In fact, by following the movement of the planets, Mayan astronomers have calculated the yearly path of Venus around the Sun with an error of only fourteen seconds per year.

Numbers are represented by bars and dots, with a dot standing for one and a bar standing for five. A picture of a seashell means zero. Numbers greater than nineteen are indicated by using the same bars and dots in different positions (the same way that the number three can mean thirty if it is put in the ten's place). The bar and dot system is simple because instead of ten different symbols (0, 1, 2, 3, 4, 5, 6, 7, 8, 9), there are only three (dot, bar, shell). And there are no fractions, which would make math class a lot easier, if there was one (the Maya don't have schools).

... the magnificent *katun* ceremony on March 18, 692, in Tikal. You will be able to stand among the thousands of spectators in the plaza and watch the nobles perform chants and rituals in a cloud of incense. At noon, the ruler, Ah Cacau, will enter wearing a spectacular quetzal feather headdress. In his hand, he will be carrying a wooden staff decorated with seashells and carved images of the gods of rulership. He will draw his own blood to link himself to the sacred calendar for the next katun.

One day is called a *kin*. Twenty kins equals a *uinal*, a time period similar to a month. Eighteen uinals (360 days) are called a *tun*. The *haab* is equal to a tun plus five days. Do the math and you'll see that a haab equals 365 days, close to the solar year. The Mayan calculation of the length of one year is 365.2420 days. That differs from modern calculations by only .0002 of a day (about seventeen seconds)!

The locals hold a celebration for each new year. Five days before the old year ends, each Mayan community gathers for a short ceremony. At the entrance to the town, a priest sets up a pottery idol that represents the god who is associated with the coming year. Townspeople gather and the priest lights incense and sacrifices an animal to the idol. Then everyone celebrates with a big feast and dancing. After the ceremony, people go straight home for the rest of the year to observe a period called Uayeb. The Maya believe this time to be particularly unlucky. It's best to avoid visiting during Uayeb because there is little to see or do.

To talk about longer periods of time, locals refer to the *katun*. One katun equals twenty tuns (or 7,200 days—that's about twenty years). After each katun passes, the Maya build and carve a katun stone. The carvings record important historical information about the katun that has just ended. You will find katun stones in many of the Mayan centers. You may even see some katun stones that mark half or quarter katun periods.

Stone monuments called stelae, carved with glyphs (intricate picture symbols), record events and information about rulers and other important people. The dates are marked from a particular starting point,

A stelae serves as both a monument and as a page in ancient Mayan history. Accounts of important events are preserved in stone.

when the Maya believe time began. The starting point on the Mayan calendar translates into 3114 B.C. on the modern calendar.

LANGUAGE LESSON

The Maya speak as many as twenty-three different languages or dialects—regional variations that have different pronunciations from other regional varieties of the same language. Many of these languages are related, but some are only as similar as, say, French and English. You will find the biggest differences between the languages spoken in the highlands and those spoken in the lowlands.

The Mayan written language consists of glyphs. Unlike other language systems in ancient America, the Mayan glyphs are not just pictures of objects. Many of them also represent specific sounds (there is a specific glyph to represent the sound "poh," for example). The bad news is that there are about eight hundred glyphs, so it may take you a while to learn them.

Mayan glyphs decorate a surface in the Temple of Inscriptions at Palenque.

At first you may think that the glyphs all look alike. However, with a little patience, you may be able to recognize some key symbols. Each glyph contains a main sign (the largest and central design) to which additions are made. It is sort of like taking a basic English word, like "arm," and adding suffixes (endings) such as "ed" or "ing" or adding prefixes (beginnings) like "dis" to change the word's meaning. Read Mayan signs beginning with the sign on the left, then the one on the top, followed by the main sign in the middle, then the one below, and finally, the one on the right.

Back TO THE FUTURE

People use glyphs in modern times, too. For example, computer programs use glyphs (called icons) to represent files, programs, and operations.

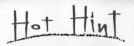

THE NAME GAME

The locals take pride in their family histories, which they trace through both the mother's and the father's side. Each person has two last names, one from the father's family and one from the mother's. In addition, a person has a private first name, given at a special naming ceremony. The first name is not made public and is seldom used, because the locals feel using a name too much reduces its power.

Boys' private names begin with "Ah," and girls' names begin with "Ix." Popular names for boys include Ah Cuy (Owl), Ah Tok (Flint Knife), and Ah Kukum (Feather). Names for girls include Ix Chan, Ix Can, and Ix Kukul. The locals also have nicknames, which are the names they use every day. Names can be quite descriptive. You may hear of people such as Stormy Sky, Lady Great Skull, Great Jaguar Paw, Smoking Squirrel, and even Curl Nose.

WHICH CITIES TO VISIT

Imposing stone temples overlook the Great Plaza at Tikal. The plaza is the center for religious and political ceremonies during ancient Mayan times.

MAYAN CENTERS

In Mayan civilization, you'll find that common people live on farms and in villages scattered across the countryside. Locals may also live in small rural villages, medium-sized towns, and in the outskirts of big cities. The middle of big Mayan cities are ceremonial centers that people visit for ceremonies, ball games, markets, and other community activities.

20

Mayan centers contain ball courts, temples, government offices, palaces, and other monuments. Each center has its own rulers and they are the only people who live there.

No matter which city you visit, you will find that the general design is the same. You will enter most towns by walking along a raised causeway, or *sacbeob* ("white road"), made of white limestone. The sacbeob connects important buildings to the ceremonial locations in the center.

The road will lead you to a large, raised platform, built from stone blocks. From here you must climb a series of steps to reach the center itself. The steps will be narrow—about eight inches high and only four inches deep—so you might have to turn your feet sideways or walk on your toes to climb them.

When you get to the top, you will be able to look across a beautiful, open plaza (square) to the large, flattop pyramid at the far end. Around the plaza, you will see other buildings, platforms, and terraces. The floor of the plaza may be painted red, the sacred color associated with life and death. The surface of the pyramid, particularly if it has been built recently, will be a dazzling, creamy white. There may be stelae arranged in a row or simply grouped at the foot of the pyramid.

You will see that the pyramid has many levels. Unlike the Egyptian pyramids, most of which are smooth-sided, Mayan pyramids have steps up the side. At the top is a temple. The steps of the pyramid are too big to climb. Passing over them, straight from the bottom to the top on one side of the structure, is a giant stairway. From a distance, it looks a little like a wheelchair ramp placed over a set of stairs.

IMPORTANT

Safety Tip

Do not climb pyramid steps. Only the highest-level priests are allowed to climb up to the stone temple at the top and step inside. Here they can gaze upon the images of the gods and the sacred writings that explain the past and foretell the future.

Along the sides of the plaza may be pyramids and temples of varying sizes. Near the entrance, you may see some longer, lower buildings, also on pyramid-shaped bases. The rulers and priests live in these buildings.

Step inside one of these buildings and you will see that the walls are usually covered with a thin layer of plaster and then painted with elaborate murals. The artist first sketches the design in a reddish tan color and then covers it with a rich black. You may be surprised at the array of colors—bright orange, pale and dark yellows, brilliant blue, a variety of greens, dark brown, and several reds and pinks. The locals create these paints from natural materials that contain color—such as plants, minerals, and clays.

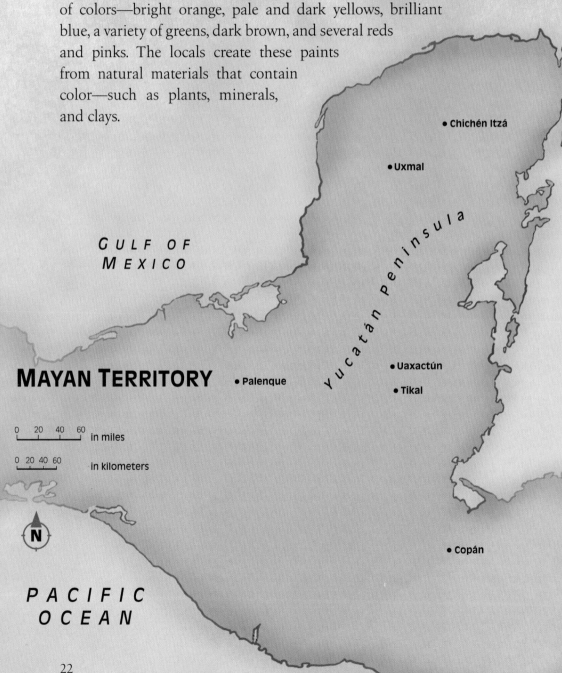

GULF OF MEXICO

• Chichén Itzá

• Uxmal

Yucatán Peninsula

MAYAN TERRITORY

• Palenque

• Uaxactún

• Tikal

0 20 40 60 in miles

0 20 40 60 in kilometers

N

• Copán

PACIFIC OCEAN

The House of the Magician at Uxmal

Uxmal

Uxmal, a city that is at its height between A.D. 800 and A.D. 950, is located in the western Yucatán—an area that will one day be part of Mexico. The largest building is more than three hundred feet long and contains twenty-four rooms. It is probably the largest and finest building in all of pre-Columbian America. The outside walls are decorated with a colorful mosaic made up of some twenty thousand pieces. The mosaics seem to identify the building as a ruling council house.

The most unusual building is the Adivino, or House of the Magician. A place where ceremonies are held, the Adivino was built so that its western stairway faces the setting sun during the summer solstice (the longest day of the year). You can reach it by climbing a very steep staircase to the templelike structure at the top of the high, round-cornered platform. The west wall of the building is made to resemble the face of a giant monster. The door to the temple is the monster's mouth.

Tikal

Tikal is one of the largest centers of the Mayan civilization during the late Classic period and is home to as many as ninety thousand people. It is located in the northern part of present-day Guatemala. At least ten thousand people live within a half hour's walk from "downtown," and another fifteen thousand to thirty thousand people live close enough to visit often.

Take time to explore the Great Plaza. This is where people gather for ceremonies and where you will find two enormous temples (at 140 feet, they are the Empire State Buildings of their time). Around the plaza, you will see gardens and groves of ramón trees. You will find eight enormous temple pyramids here, some rising more than two hundred feet into the air, as well as many smaller buildings. Don't miss the lavish hieroglyphic carvings everywhere you look, particularly on the wooden beams called lintels that bridge the pyramid doorways.

The Hieroglyphic Stairway at Copán contains thousands of glyphs describing the history of Copán.

COPÁN

Copán is a major center of ten thousand to twenty thousand people in the southeastern lowlands. It is worth visiting for its spectacular architecture and sculptures. If you are able to visit between A.D. 628 and A.D. 820, you'll catch the center when it's really thriving. Copán is a center for astronomical studies. The city even hosts an important conference of scholar-priests in 765. Virtually everywhere you look you will see sculptures of gods, animals, humans, and mythological beings. While you may see such work elsewhere, the sculptures and stone reliefs are particularly elaborate here. Due to its altitude—more than two thousand feet above sea level—Copán has a cooler climate than some other Mayan centers.

If you can, visit the Hieroglyphic Stairway during its dedication in 756. Consisting of a series of seventy-two steps, the stairway climbs the side of a temple near the ball court. Note the large, sculpted animal

The Temple of Inscriptions at Palenque rises into a hillside.

figure that appears in the middle of every twelfth step. The front of each step is decorated with as many as two thousand individual glyphs. It is well worth getting a local translation of the glyphs' message, as the steps become worn in later years, and archaeologists will be unable to decipher them.

PALENQUE

Palenque is located in the northern part of the highlands on a jungle tributary (a stream feeding into a larger river) of the Usumacinta River. Be sure to check out the beautiful, painted panels on many of the buildings—the paint will wear off in the years to come.

Pay particular attention to the Temple of Inscriptions, located at the top of a terraced platform. It was built to honor Palenque's greatest ruler, Pacal, who died in 683. Across the front of the temple, you will see five doorways. (It is highly unusual to have so many doors right next to each other.) What you can't see is Pacal's tomb, which is hidden in an underground chamber beneath the platform. Don't even bother trying to get to it. The locals have closed the crypt with a huge stone block, filled the chamber and the stairs with rubble, and sealed the temple floor with large slabs of stone.

Palenque is one of the finest Mayan cities and has excellent sculptures. This is due in part to the skill of local craftspeople and to the quality of the local stone. The fineness of the stone also explains the quality of the stucco (a plaster material) work here. While in Copán, you may find strong, sharp designs carved into stone. At Palenque the locals often draw smooth, flowing lines in the soft stucco. Unfortunately, Palenque is among the first Mayan cities in the south to lose its power and go into decline, so be sure to visit between 642 and 783.

UAXACTÚN

Uaxactún is about twenty-five miles north of Tikal but is quite a bit smaller. You may want to drop by for a visit anyway to view the astronomical observatory. The buildings are designed in a unique way. Stand on the west stairway of the pyramid during the autumnal equinox (a twenty-four-hour period with equal hours of day and night) on September 23. Look toward the three temples on the opposite side and you will see the Sun rise directly above the middle temple. The same thing happens on the vernal (spring) equinox on March 21. On the

Now Hear This

Traders are respected throughout the Mayan civilization. They don't have to pay taxes, and the locals go out of their way to help traders on their journeys. Mayan traders exchange ideas with other Mayan groups. They also share ideas with nearby cultures, such as the Olmec, a people from the gulf coastal plain to the west. For example, the Mayans may learn different patterns for weaving or new ways to prepare foods.

shortest day of the year, December 21, the Sun rises at the outside corner of the temple on the south side. On the longest day of the year, June 21, the Sun rises on the outside corner of the temple on the north side.

CHICHÉN ITZÁ

If you decide to travel later than the Classic period of Mayan civilization, be sure to visit Chichén Itzá (its original Mayan name). This spectacular center in north-central Yucatán covers approximately ten square miles. Although part of Chichén Itzá had been built in the 400s, it was abandoned near the end of the 600s. Most of Chichén Itzá is built in the late 800s or early 900s.

Chichén Itzá is home to many fascinating buildings. An unusual round structure on top of two rectangular platforms serves as an observation chamber. Through square openings in the walls, you can watch the movements of the Sun and Moon.

Chichén Itzá also has at least seven ball courts, including one huge court—measuring 545 feet by 223 feet—that may be the largest in all of Mesoamerica (a region of Central America including Mexico, Guatemala, El Salvador, Belize, and Honduras). But unlike the courts designed earlier, the walls at the Great Ball Court at Chichén Itzá are completely vertical. Halfway down the court, a single ring is set near the top of the wall. So it's entirely possible that the game you watch here will vary from games you may see elsewhere in the Mayan civilization.

Handy WORDS & PHRASES

Chichén Itzá means "opening of the wells of the Itzá." The area has two large wells (one of which is a particularly important site for sacrifices). The Itzá people are Maya living in the Yucatán region.

(Facing page) *The ancient Mayan observatory at Chichén Itzá is called El Caracol. It has windows that align with the planet Venus and the Sun at certain times of the year. The Maya hold festivals when Venus and the Sun are in view.*

MONEY MATTERS

Green pods grow on the cacao tree's trunk. Once the pods ripen, the beans inside are harvested and dried.

A CACAO BEAN FOR YOUR THOUGHTS

The Maya don't use money, so you won't find any coins or bills here. However, you can get anything you need by bartering (trading) in the marketplace, as the locals do. The Maya trade what's readily available to

them for things that they can't grow or find locally. For example, the highland Maya have copal (a material used for incense), flint, alum, obsidian, jade, quetzal feathers, and cochineal (an insect that, when crushed, provides color for dye or paint). They trade these with the lowland Maya for cotton, salt, honey, wax, seashells, dried fish, smoked deer, and cacao.

Cacao beans—the source of chocolate—are made into a very expensive chocolate drink used only during ceremonies. The locals grow the beans in their own household gardens and also cultivate large groves of cacao trees. The tree only grows well in some areas. Pests or drought can reduce crops, so the beans are quite valuable. Here, chocolate is money. And it actually does grow on trees!

Prices
OF COMMON GOODS

1 rabbit—10 cacao beans

1 pumpkin—4 cacao beans

1 adult male slave—100 cacao beans (enough to make about 25 cups of chocolate)

31

HOW TO GET AROUND

BY LAND

The locals haven't yet discovered the wheel, so you will probably be traveling on foot. The road system, which was created from age-old trade routes, is very good. Within cities and towns, roads connect major buildings. Roads extend from one city center to the next, making travel on foot easier.

As you travel between cities, you may even find distance markers and rest stops along the way. If you come upon a "traveler's house," feel free to build a fire with the wood, eat the maize, or use other supplies on hand. The nearest village appoints someone to stock the shelters for travelers and visiting traders.

Attendants transport their ruler in a litter (portable chair). Trumpeters accompany him.

It's easy to visit lots of different areas on foot. You will have to carry your stuff on your back when you walk. The Maya have no horses, mules, or other beasts of burden. Mayan traders walk great distances, with their goods strapped around their heads or chests.

If you plan to buy souvenirs along the way, you may want to hire porters. These servants will transport your belongings in cloth packs on their backs. In your travels, you may even see whole caravans of porters carrying goods for trade (it's the Mayan version of Federal Express).

As in most cultures, the rich and powerful travel with more style and comfort than the common folk. Slaves may carry the ruler and others of high rank in a litter, a portable chair or bed. The ruler will

Although people in India are using the wheel as early as 3000 B.C., Mesoamerican cultures never did. This may be, in part, because they had no draft animals for pulling wheeled carts and saw no use for the wheel.

probably be followed by a large number of servants. It is unlikely that you, as a common traveler, will be able to talk anyone into letting you ride in a litter.

BY WATER

You may be able to visit some areas by canoe. The Mayan canoe, or *chem*, is carved from a single tree trunk, usually cedar. Many of the important centers in the southern lowlands are on major rivers. Some central lowland towns, including El Mirador, Tikal, and Uaxactún, lie

between waterways. These centers make ideal rest stops—you'll be tired after carrying the canoe from one body of water to the next!

The Maya also use oceangoing canoes to travel thousands of miles along the coastal waters. The inexperienced visitor should not try this without a local guide. Some of these vessels are large enough to carry twenty to thirty people, plus items for trade. You may see feather banners attached to long poles along the shore. These are markers that help sea travelers determine their location.

SIDE TRIP TRIVIA In 1502 Christopher Columbus, on his fourth and last voyage to the Americas, encounters a Mayan trading canoe off the northern coast of what will become Honduras. This is the first recorded contact between Europeans and the Maya.

A reproduction of an ancient Mayan fresco shows scenes of daily life from a coastal village. Sailors in canoes patrol the coastline, protecting the village from enemy armies.

LOCAL CUSTOMS & MANNERS

WHAT YOU CAN EXPECT FROM THE LOCALS

The Maya tend to be short and strongly built. The women average about four feet eight inches tall, and the men average five feet one inch. So if you are tall, you may draw some looks.

The Maya have straight black hair and coppery-brown skin. You will notice that the locals (particularly those of high rank) have large, flat foreheads that slope backward. This is considered a mark of beauty, but it's a look that does not come naturally. During infancy, when a child's skull is still somewhat soft, the parents place the baby's head between a pair of boards. They bind the boards tightly around the head. The boards will remain in place for several days. When the priest removes the boards, they will have permanently reshaped the skull.

Some good news is that big noses are definitely in here. Crossed eyes are also quite desirable. In fact, mothers often hang little resin balls from their children's bangs and between the eyes to encourage them to look inward.

BEING A KID

Children spend most of their time imitating grown-ups. Boys follow their fathers into the fields to learn farming. Girls help their mothers with home tasks, learning how to prepare maize and make tortillas.

Parents teach children about teamwork, obedience, and respect for Mayan priests and nobles. One of the most important lessons children learn is how to obtain good luck. Children attend temple ceremonies and stand guard on unlucky days. (Locals believe that the movements of the stars and planets bring good luck or bad luck.) Reading, writing, and arithmetic are important only for children of the highest social class.

This relief portrait of a Mayan woman shows her flattened forehead, elaborate hairdo, and facial tattoos—all signs of beauty in ancient Mayan culture.

37

Some modern-day experts believe this painting shows a marriage negotiation. A ruler, with attendants, arranges a deal while two women are seated behind a partition (on right). Below, a dwarf guards a mirror and three sacks of goods to trade.

Remember that the Maya do not have schools. But boys and young men do live apart from their families in special houses where they study religion, social skills, and battle techniques.

Sons of rulers prepare themselves to rule in the future. They learn the ways of the village people, who they will one day rule. By the age of twelve, they might already have jobs sweeping the temple courtyards or leading groups of dancers. This is good practice for leading important religious ceremonies and other rituals when they are older.

When children are three or four, their parents attach a bead to the hair on the top of a boy's head and tie a red shell on a string around a girl's waist to symbolize childhood and purity. To remove the bead or the shell before the child reaches puberty is highly improper. When boys reach the age of fourteen and girls turn twelve, they go through a special coming-of-age ceremony. At the ceremony, priests and elders explain the duties of adulthood. The priests remove the bead attached to the boy's head or the shell tied around the girl's waist. Children who have gone through this ceremony are considered adults and are free to marry.

Boys usually marry when they're eighteen, and girls marry when they're fourteen. Parents arrange most marriages, often with the help of a matchmaker. The main consideration is not love or even money. Instead, matchmakers try to match couples whose astrological (zodiac) signs work well together. The wedding date is also critical because it could mean good or bad luck for the couple. According to tradition, the groom's family gives the bride's parents clothing and other valuables, such as cacao beans or spondylus shells. The groom must live with and work for the bride's parents for five to seven years after the marriage. The newly married couple does not take a honeymoon trip.

Divorce is common here. All it takes is for the husband or the wife to declare that the marriage is over. Both are then free to marry someone else.

SOCIAL STRUCTURE

The Maya have a small, elite group of wealthy people with a lot of power. The rulers, priests, and nobles are born into the elite group. They will marry people within the elite group, and their children will also be of that group. At the top are the *k'ul ahau* (king) and his family. The k'ul ahau holds all political, economic, and religious power. The locals believe that the king provides a direct link to the gods.

Most locals are not part of the elite group. Commoners are farmers who raise crops, craftspeople who make goods to trade in the market-place, and servants or workers who keep the centers running. Servants

TAKE IT from a Local

Mayan rulers pass power from the father to the oldest son. Sometimes the power passes to the son of the king's daughter. In these cases, the woman may act as a royal power broker, since it is her father—not her husband's father—who was the previous king.

It is rare for a woman to become a ruler, but it happens. For instance, Lady Kanal Ikal, daughter of Chan Bahlum I, becomes the first female ruler of Palenque in 583 when there are no male heirs to the throne. Her son takes control twenty years later.

39

and workers hope their service will persuade the gods to bring successful crops and good luck.

You will see a big difference between the lives of ordinary farmers and royalty. But families here can gain or lose power. As new ruling families come into power, others lose power. Common folk have also been known to improve their standing in society through successful business ventures or election to religious or government office.

From Dawn to Dusk

In the morning, women start preparing tortillas and beans for breakfast. The men usually spend this time outside, praying for good hunting, rain for the crops, or other daily needs. After breakfast, the men will head for the fields or go hunting for deer, turkey, or rabbits. Mayan women spend much of their time preparing maize tortillas, an important part of most Mayan meals. Maize has tough, fibrous kernels. Mayan women must soak the dried corn kernels in a pot of lime and water, cook the corn over a stone hearth until the kernels soften, and then grind the dried corn with stone tools called the mano and metate, to make it soft enough for tortillas. The ground corn, called *zacan*, is then allowed to stand until later in the morning.

The ancient Mayans use manos and metates to grind maize for tortillas. This technology is widely used throughout the Americas.

Warm weather year-round allows Mayan farmers to raise a wide range of interesting and nutritional foods. In fact, the ancient Mayan civilization offers more variety of food than ancient Europe at this same period.

To make tortillas, a Mayan woman will put a round griddle on the stone hearth to heat. She will use her hands to flatten the corn mush into a tortilla. She then bakes the tortilla on the griddle. When the tortilla puffs up, she flattens it again with her hand and puts it in a gourd to keep it hot. Mayan women soak and heat beans to serve with the tortillas.

Men usually take their lunch with them in the morning, but if they are in fields close by, their wives may bring food out to them. You will see farmers' wives in the fields, helping their husbands sow and cultivate crops, too. The men work long days clearing fields, planting seeds, and harvesting crops by hand. The Maya grow corn, cotton, squash, chile peppers, and beans. Between the planting season and the harvest, Mayan farmers help build limestone temples in the Mayan centers.

Wives often have a bath ready for their husbands when they come in from the fields. Bathing is a big chore, so don't expect a fresh bath every day. First the women heat the water in pots. Then they carry the pots to a wooden bathtub. It may take several pots of water to fill the tub. An alternative is the public steam baths, which you will find in cities such as Tikal. Women, men, and children also bathe in cenotes, deep limestone pits that fill with rainwater. But take care—some cenotes are reserved for sacrifices. Steer clear of those with long clifflike walls that drop many feet down to the water's surface. Victims are thrown over the sides.

The locals eat the main meal of the day—usually tortillas, chiles, and beans—shortly before sunset. Mayan families do not eat together. The men and boys are served first. Women and girls eat afterward. You will eat sitting on a stool or on a mat spread on the floor. It is considered proper to wash before and after meals. Your host will offer you soap made from the roots of the soapberry tree.

After dinner, the locals usually talk with friends or neighbors or work around the house. After dark, the Maya use pine splinters as candles. The women may spin plant fibers into cloth or weave beautiful, intricate cloth

In this terra-cotta (baked clay) sculpture, a Mayan woman weaves fabric on a loom.

on a simple hand loom. If you see a woman walking to market, look carefully. Notice that she spins cotton into thread on weighted spindles as she walks! Women also craft beautiful pottery by hand.

The men may repair tools. The family will eat a light meal—probably just tortillas and beans—at eight or nine o'clock, just before bed.

LOCAL MANNERS

Manners are generally relaxed here. For example, at the dinner table the Maya don't use utensils. Instead, they roll up a tortilla and scoop up food. At the end of the meal, they simply eat their spoons.

There are some formalities you should observe. For example, it is customary to bring gifts such as shells or cacao beans when you visit people. Children are taught to show respect to adults. When meeting a person of the elite class, repeat the person's title over and over. When someone is talking, you should make small noises to indicate that you are paying attention and want to hear more, much like we nod or say "mmhmmm" in conversation.

If you are a male, and a young woman turns her back to you, don't be offended. Young women are taught to be modest in the presence of a man. They are supposed to turn their backs and step aside to allow a man to pass. When giving a man a drink, they are supposed to lower their eyes.

SLAVERY

You will notice that slavery is an accepted part of life here. Slaves may be born into slavery, but most slaves are captured during war. Slavery can also be a punishment for certain crimes. For instance, if someone steals from another person and cannot return the goods or pay for them, the thief must work for the victim as a slave until the debt is paid. (Sometimes this can be an entire lifetime.)

A family with severe financial problems may sell one or more children into slavery. Orphans may also end up as slaves. In wealthy households, slaves do most of the hard work. Male slaves paddle boats, carry heavy loads on their backs, and perform other unpleasant tasks. Female slaves grind corn, draw water, dye thread, and help with other household chores.

Slaves have no real life of their own because they can be bought and sold at any time. If a master dies, it is not unusual for his slaves to be killed and buried with him.

This relief shows a captive slave. His arms are bound behind him with a rope.

LOCAL BELIEFS

The Maya believe that there are thirteen layers of Upperworld above Earth and nine layers of underworld below Earth. However, they see the three regions (Upperworld, Earth, and Underworld) as one universe, with no boundaries separating them. The natural and the supernatural realms blend together.

The locals believe that gods stand at the four corners of Earth and hold up the sky. These four corners are considered sacred and are associated with different kinds of power, usually related to the forces of nature. For example, Ah Kin, the sun god, rises in the east. He brings blessings to growing things and provides warmth and fertility. Even when he sinks into the Underworld (as the Sun sets), he brings blessings to things, such as buried seeds.

If you want to understand the Mayan belief system, read *Popol Vuh*, the book of the Quiché Maya, a group of people who live in the highlands of what will one day become Guatemala. Although the Maya believe that the universe has been created and destroyed several times, *Popol Vuh* provides a creation story for this world.

According to *Popol Vuh*, the Hero Twins—Hunahpu and Xbalanque—go to Xibalbá (the Underworld), where the gods of death

In a scene from the Quiché Mayan book Popol Vuh, *the Hero Twins* (far left) *use whistles to call birds, while two women dress Hun Hunahpu* (center), *the god of maize, after he is brought back to life.*

force the twins to play a series of ball games for their lives. In the end, the Hero Twins sacrifice themselves by fire. The death gods grind the twins' bones and throw the powder into the river. But the twins are reborn. They return to Xibalbá and take revenge upon the gods of death. The twins become the main celestial bodies (the Sun and Venus). Each day they reenact their descent into Xibalbá (as the setting Sun) and their escape (as Venus, the morning or evening star). This story is

Hot Hint

You may have heard stories such as those in *Popol Vuh* referred to as "myths." However, that term would insult the locals, who believe in these ancient stories as strongly as many modern people believe accounts from sacred books such as the Bible, the Torah, or the Koran.

the basis of many Mayan customs, including the ball game and the idea of rebirth through sacrifice.

THE GODS

The Maya believe that all things—living or not—have an unseen power or spirit. They believe that some spirits reside in rocks, trees, and other objects, where they have no particular shape or form of their own. Other spirits, the locals believe, are gods that take the form of animals or humans.

The locals have gods of war, childbirth, sleep, dance, and even hunger. The Maya also believe there are gods for the Sun, rain, the North Star, maize, and other important parts of the universe.

Some locals believe that Hunab Ku is the chief of the gods. Most people will tell you that his son, Itzamná, is the Lord of Life. You may see images of Itzamná (he is shown as a wrinkled old man) with his wife, the goddess Ix Chel. These two gave birth to all the other gods and goddesses. You will find that there are many gods and goddesses. Each one may play several roles, have more than one name, and be pictured in different ways.

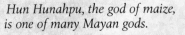

Hun Hunahpu, the god of maize, is one of many Mayan gods.

WATCHING THE SKIES

The locals believe that all of the deities (gods) work together to control the regular cycles of birth, aging, and death. They also control the dawning and setting of the Sun and the movements of heavenly bodies—all of which mark the passage of time. This orderly pattern, they believe, assures that life will continue.

The locals have a keen interest in astronomy. They study the constellations, the movements of the planets, and even the Milky Way galaxy. These celestial objects help them understand the universe and the creation of life. In fact, many of the images you see on Mayan pottery, stones, and paintings represent astronomical events.

You will not find telescopes here. All the same, the Maya have sophisticated systems for watching the skies. For example, Mayan astronomers set up a series of crossed sticks at the top of a pyramid. With the naked eye, they can then align a distant object in the sky with the center of the sticks. This system allows them to accurately observe and record the movements of planets, the Sun, and the Moon.

THE IMPORTANCE OF SACRIFICE

Sacrifice—offerings to the gods—is an important part of religious worship here. To cure illness or ward off minor problems, the locals may offer a gift of food, pottery, or the hearts of large animals (such as jaguars or crocodiles) to the gods. At special times, such as the birth of

A relief from the city of Yaxchilán shows the ruler Shield Jaguar and his wife, Lady Xoc. She is pulling a barbed rope through her tongue in a bloodletting ceremony.

Don't
Miss

. . . sacred rituals where the Maya use bloodletting to celebrate victory in battle, to communicate with ancestors, or to honor an heir ascending to the throne. The Maya use thorns, sharpened flints, or stingray spines to pierce their tongues or the skin between their fingers. They then sprinkle the blood on idols (wood, stone, or clay statues of gods) or let it drip on bark paper. They burn the bark paper, believing that the smoke will carry the blood to the gods.

an heir to the throne, the end of a katun, or the beginning of a war, Mayan rulers offer their own blood to the gods. This ritual is called bloodletting. The locals believe members of royalty are a link between the common person and the gods. Bloodletting accompanies many religious ceremonies, festivals, and holidays such as New Year celebrations.

In times of great need, such as drought or famine, the locals offer human lives. The Maya believe that human sacrifice brings rain, fertility, and the continuation of the Mayan people and their universe. In one type of human sacrifice, priests throw a person, often a child, from a high ledge or into a cenote, which may contain water. In some cases, the child survives by swimming or holding on to the wall. The next day, the locals lower a rope and bring the child up. They believe the gods will have spoken to the child, who will be able to answer questions about the future. If the child dies, the locals believe the child was simply taken by the gods to the heavens or to the underworld.

Slaves are often chosen for sacrifice to the gods. Rich lords sacrifice orphan slaves, particularly if the child's mother was also a slave. When the locals take prisoners of war, they sacrifice the prisoners that are higher-ranking officers to the gods. The lower-ranking prisoners become the slaves of the soldiers who captured them.

The locals sometimes perform a more formal kind of human sacrifice. They take off the person's clothes, paint the body blue (the color of sacrifice), and place an elaborate, peaked headdress on the person's head. Then they lead the person to a special place (often the top of a pyramid), where they lay the person on a stone that curves upward in

The walls of the Sacred Cenote, a sacrificial cenote, at Chichén Itzá drop about forty feet to the water below.

Prisoners await their fate during a human sacrifice in Bonampak.

the middle to raise the chest. Then assistants hold the arms and feet, stretching the person over the stone. A special priest called the *nacom* plunges a knife into the chest, reaches in, pulls out the still-beating heart, and hands it to the officiating priest, called the *chilan*. The chilan smears the blood on an idol and then throws the body to the courtyard below. Priests of lower rank skin the body, except for the hands and feet, which will be saved for the chilan. The chilan then takes off his ceremonial clothing and wears the human skin while performing a solemn dance with the spectators.

If the individual being sacrificed was a brave soldier, his body may be divided up and eaten by the nobles. The locals see this as a way to gain some of his power or to show off their own. As a spectator, you may be offered some as well.

Another essential part of religious ceremony is incense (material that gives off smoke and a pleasant odor when burned). The priest's assistant will prepare the incense and put it on small specially designed boards or in pottery containers.

DEATH & BEYOND

The locals believe in life after death. Those who die during a noble deed—such as women who die giving birth, warriors who are killed in battle, people who are sacrificed to the gods, and those who commit suicide—are thought to be rewarded in the afterlife. Evil people are condemned to an afterlife of never-ending cold, hunger, and torment in a demon-filled underworld.

If someone of great importance dies, the locals place the dead person in a small, stone-lined vault. Then they build a temple or pyramid over it, leaving a passageway to the tomb. They put many items in the tomb, such as furniture, tools, brightly painted pottery, and carved jade beads. They may bury the person in a shroud (burial garment) with jewels, clothing, weapons, a favorite dog, and even slaves—complete with the tools they will need to serve their master in the afterlife. They fill the dead person's mouth with ground maize and jade beads so that he or she will not be without food or valuable objects to trade in the afterlife.

WHAT TO WEAR

A Mayan noble wears an intricate headdress and jewelry.

CLOTHES

If you are male, you will have to wear an elaborate type of loincloth called an *ex*. To put on an ex, wind an eight- to ten-foot-long strip of ten-inch-wide cotton cloth around your waist several times. Pass it between your legs, allowing the flaps at either end of the cloth to hang down in front and back. If you want to be really stylish, use a second and wider strip of cloth and roll it around your waist into a really thick belt. Look for material with colorful embroidery or other decoration. Some ex garments have exquisite feather work or are decorated with ornaments. In general, people of higher rank wear the most ornate exes. Since the climate is quite warm, an ex should suit you fine. But if you like, you can add a capelike garment called a *pati*. Patis range from the simplest cotton square, draped over the shoulders of a common man, to magnificent capes made from the iridescent tail feathers of the quetzal. These brilliant blue-green feathers can be up to three feet long. They are highly prized and usually reserved for people of the highest rank. If you choose a simple cloth pati, you can also use it to cover your bed at night, the way many locals do. Other patis may be made from the hides of deer, leopard, jaguar, or even snake. Jaguar skins are reserved for people of the highest rank, and tourists cannot purchase them.

Women here wear a cotton garment similar to a skirt. Women of high rank will have skirts with decorative knots or fringe. Women may wear nothing on top (the climate is warm, remember). In coastal areas, women wear a skirt and a folded square of cloth tied under their armpits. Young children usually wear nothing at all. As a tourist, you may feel uncomfortable in the traditional garb. A straight, simple dress may be the answer. The dress may be no more than a sort of long sack, tied together at the hips, but will be woven or embroidered in brilliant colors.

This statuette of a female fertility goddess wears a typical Mayan-style skirt.

A carving of ancient Mayan sandals

The locals dye thread and cloth with plant and animal extracts. They use brazilwood, iron oxide, or cochineal insects to make red dyes. Avocado fruit makes green dyes, blackberries or the ink from mollusks make dark purple, and carbon makes black. The locals often use urine to prepare the dyes.

It would not be at all unusual to see the locals wearing nothing on their feet. The locals have thick layers of skin on the bottoms of their feet, from years of going barefoot. Your feet will be much too tender to go without shoes for long, so you'll need to get yourself a pair of sandals. These generally have high ankle pieces (almost like boots) or may be laced up the ankle. The sandals here have two straps between the toes— one between the big toe and the second toe, and the other between the third and fourth toes. The common people wear

SIDE TRIP TRIVIA

If you visit Europe at this time, you will find that the locals there also add urine to coloring sources, such as berries or wood, to make a fabric dye that will permanently color fabric.

sandals made from deer hide tied with hemp cords. People of higher rank may wear versions that are much more elaborate. Their sandals have braided straps, multiple ties, or decorated heelpieces.

HAIR

Women's hairstyles tend to be simple. They wear their hair long in a ponytail flowing from the top of the head. Sometimes they may braid or decorate their hair with ornaments. Both males and females wear hairstyles that draw attention to their flattened foreheads. Men burn off the hair at the top of their heads to make a bare spot. They wear the rest of their hair long. They braid it and wind it around their heads or gather it into a wide ponytail. They sometimes use string to tie lots of mini-ponytails around the head. A man might also pull all of his hair into a big ponytail on top of his head and tie it with a piece of cloth. Below the big ponytail, the man might wear several mini-ponytails, each held by an ornamental band. Even the poorest people wear their hair long and neatly braided. Among the Maya, slaves are the only ones who wear their hair short. If your hair is short, you may want to go for a turban or headdress, as short hair will seem odd to the locals.

This man wears a typical Mayan hairdo. The hair is swept up in a ponytail and pulled away from the face with a small headdress.

A priest wears a ceremonial headdress.

For men, the headdress is the most popular hair accessory. Like other articles of clothing, the style and quality of the headdress shows the rank of its owner. The wooden framework of the headdress may be shaped like the head of a jaguar, a snake, a bird, or a god. The frame is then covered with jaguar skin, carved jade, and brilliant feathers to create the look of a huge feathered crest. The headdress a ruler wears may be larger than the man himself.

BEAUTY

Don't be surprised if you see the locals wearing some unusual items as jewelry. Jaguar teeth and claws and crocodile teeth are quite popular. The Maya wear nose ornaments, ear decorations, and lip plugs—all made from bone, wood, shells, jade, obsidian, or feathers. They also like to wear jewelry around their necks (as collars or necklaces), wrists, ankles, legs (just below their knees), and on their heads. And that's just the men. Even the poorest people wear earrings and necklaces. None of the jewelry is metal, however. That's because the Maya do not have copper, silver, or gold.

Older children have their earlobes, septum (the piece of skin that separates your nostrils), lips, and nostrils pierced. The holes created by ear piercing can become quite large. Over time, the locals insert larger and larger plugs made from wood, bone, jade, or shell into the holes. Eventually the holes become large enough to pass an egg through.

Body paint is popular, but you'll want to choose the color carefully. Some colors have great significance. For example, unless you would like to be the main attraction at a human sacrifice, you'll want to avoid blue. Some colors or patterns show the status of the person wearing the paint. For example, unmarried men paint themselves black. Warriors paint themselves red and black, and prisoners and slaves are painted with black and white stripes. Men and women often anoint themselves with sweet-smelling red ointment, which makes them smell nice for several days.

Tattoos are very popular. Both men and women tattoo their faces as well as their bodies with elaborate designs and patterns. The tattoo artist paints on the design, then cuts the skin so that the coloring remains in the design. This process is not for the faint of heart. Getting a tattoo is so painful that artists do only a little at a time. Unfortunately, antibiotics have not yet been invented. The person being tattooed can become ill from the infections that sometimes result.

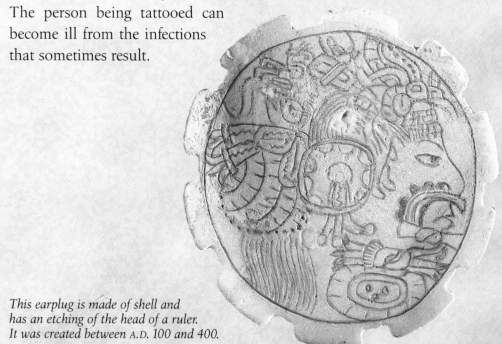

This earplug is made of shell and has an etching of the head of a ruler. It was created between A.D. *100 and 400.*

The locals decorate their teeth, too. First, they file each of their front teeth to a sharp point. Then they slip thin, flat plates made from colorful stones or shells over these teeth. The sharpened teeth grip the plates and help keep them in place. The Maya use obsidian (for black plates), jade (for green), or pyrite (for gold).

As with the clothing, you can usually tell how important a person is by how fancy his or her decorations are. You can easily pick out the area's ruler or *halach uinic*. He will probably have tattoos all over his body and face. His left nostril will have a large pierced hole, which will contain a jewel, usually a topaz. Huge earrings will hang from his pierced ears, and his teeth will be jade-plated. His head will have been carefully shaped from birth so that the top of his skull nearly comes to a point.

WHAT TO SEE & DO

Sunlight bathes the Governor's Palace at Uxmal.

THE GOVERNOR'S PALACE AT UXMAL

If you have a hard time identifying the planets and stars in the night sky at home, go to the Governor's Palace at Uxmal. Uxmal is located in the northwestern part of the Yucatán Peninsula. The palace is easy to spot. Most of the city is built in a north to south direction. But the palace was built facing the southeast so that its doorway would face a pyramid three miles away. If you visit when the planet Venus is last seen as the "morning star"—the locals will be able to tell you when this is—and you are able to get permission from the palace priests, you may be able to see a spectacular sight. If you stand so that you can view the pyramid through the palace doorway, you will see Venus rise, as if by magic, precisely over the point of the pyramid.

BONAMPAK

Bonampak is a thriving Mayan city built into a terraced hillside in the southeastern part of what will one day become Mexico. Many of the buildings are painted red, symbolizing blood and its sacred connection to the gods. If you visit in 790 or 791, you may be able to attend the ceremony honoring the heir to Bonampak's throne. At this important event, priests dedicate a building that contains spectacular murals of the ceremony. The murals also show scenes of a dramatic battle in which the heir's father and Bonampak's current ruler, Chan Muan, is victorious.

Handy WORDS & PHRASES

The name Bonampak comes from the Mayan words for "painted wall."

The ceremony features much trumpeting and celebrating. The wealthy lords wear their finest costumes, complete with heavy jade pendants, spondylus shells, and amazing headdresses. Expect a ceremonial procession, with members of the royal court wearing elaborate costumes. Musicians will play gourd rattles, wooden drums, and turtle shells. The highlight is the dramatic bloodletting ritual, which is not recommended for the squeamish.

THE TEMPLE OF KUKULCAN

If you postpone your trip to the late 900s and visit during the spring or fall equinox, be sure to go to the Temple of Kukulcan at Chichén Itzá. It is a seventy-nine-foot-high structure with four stairways, one set on

A group of musicians playing gourd rattles leads a ceremonial procession.

each of the temple's four sides. At sunset, stand where you will have a good view of the temple's north stairs (there will be many other visitors waiting to see this event). As the Sun sets, the shadow that falls on the temple looks like a snake slithering down the north stairs. For locals, it is more than just entertainment. They believe the snake shadow on the steps is a sacred appearance of Kukulcan, the feathered serpent god. He brings both good and bad omens (signs of good or bad luck).

Notice the road, which is more than thirty feet wide, that heads away from the Temple of Kukulcan. It extends nine hundred feet and leads directly to the sacrificial cenote, into which offerings are thrown. This cenote is a large and deep natural limestone pool. If you visit during a drought, you may see a child thrown into the cenote as an offering to the rain god. At other times, locals throw in offerings such as pottery, shells, and precious stones.

CAVES

Caves are often important sources of water. The locals also consider them a sign of Earth's fundamental power and believe that the caves have political and spiritual importance. You will find caves in many

Mayan centers, as the locals often choose areas with caves as sites for settlement. The twenty-two caves at Dos Pilas (in modern-day Guatemala) have passages extending seven miles. A cave under the El Duende Pyramid features a huge underground lake. If you go to the Bat Palace, a shrine located at the top of a hill at Dos Pilas, you will find the entrance to a cave. An underground passageway connects this cave to the one at El Duende.

Religious ceremonies in caves often draw people from all over Mayan civilization and sometimes even people from other Mesoamerican cultures. If you wish to attend, you should bring a small offering such as a pottery bowl or a small statue. Toss it over the edge of the sacred cenote inside the cave as an offering to the gods.

SPECIAL EVENTS

Since the locals hold a festival every twenty days (remember, that's the Mayan version of a month), chances are you will see at least one during your trip. You will find the festivities right in the town center. Although the festivals are religious events, they are far from solemn. People throw flowers, exchange gifts, and generally have a blast.

In the courtyard, you will see many men dressed in elaborate loincloths and head-dresses. The priests may be dressed as gods, wearing feathered robes and fantastic masks. They perform spectacular ceremonies, which sometimes end with a public sacrifice.

Many ceremonies begin with fasts and other personal sacrifices. Fasting usually involves following strict rules on how much or whether to eat meat, salt, and chile peppers. The Maya fast in order to purify themselves for the ceremony. Priests and people who assist with the ceremony are required to fast. But it is voluntary for everyone else. If you choose to fast and then break your fast, it is considered a great sin.

On festival days, the city leaps to life. The plaza fills with thousands of people in colorful clothing. Buyers and sellers arrive and begin trading items such as jade beads, pottery, cloth, and cacao beans.

At religious events, music, singing, and dancing abound. The dances are not just for fun. They bring to life the history, beliefs, and hopes of the local people. The movements of the dance put the participants into a sort of trance. Groups as large as eight hundred people—men and women—may perform a dance without a single person being out of step.

Don't Miss

. . . a dance called the Colomché, the game of reeds. A large group of dancers forms a circle, and two dancers move to the center to the beat of the music. One holds a handful of reeds and dances standing up, while the other crouches. The dancer holding the reeds throws them with all his strength at the other, who has to catch them using a small stick. When they are finished, they join the circle, and two other dancers take their place.

(Facing page) *This scene shows a ruler (on right) dancing in a ceremony while attendants watch.*

WHERE TO FIND SPORTS & RECREATION

POK-A-TOK

If you have played volleyball, you may have an advantage playing the Mayan ball game called *pok-a-tok*. Opposing teams volley a hard rubber ball that's about the size of a volleyball back and forth. They try to knock it into certain areas on the sloping sides of the court without letting it hit the ground. But here is the tricky part—players aren't allowed to use their hands or feet to move the ball. Instead, players must bump the ball with their hips, elbows, or other body parts to prevent it from hitting the ground. Although players wear protective padding, the game can be quite rough.

Mayan ballplayers wear elaborate costumes, headdresses, and lots of padding. Keeping the ball in the air is no easy task—the ball weighs about eight pounds.

In one version of the game, a stone ring with an opening perpendicular to the ground is set into the middle of each of the two side walls. The object is to get the rubber ball through one of the rings using only the elbow, wrist, or hip. Better hope that you are not there on one of the rare days when a player actually makes that shot, however. According to an ancient rule, the winning player gets all of the spectators' clothing and jewelry. So if you see a shot go in, run for the exit with the locals. You'll have to be quick to outrun the player's friends, who will chase you to try to collect what is due.

You may see some of the locals gambling on the outcome of the game. People might bet turquoise, slaves, cornfields, or even their homes on the outcome of a single game.

Pok-a-tok isn't just a sport. It's also a sacred ceremony that the locals take very seriously. To them, the ball game is an opening into life after death and a way for the locals to celebrate victory in war. They force captured enemy soldiers to reenact the battle on the ball court. At the

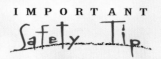

Don't volunteer to be a team captain. The locals take pok-a-tok so seriously that the losing captain is sometimes sacrificed.

end, the locals sacrifice the soldiers.

If you are used to relying on television or computers for entertainment, you'll have to change your thinking here. Toys tend to be simple. Kids have lots of free time, and they play with balls and dolls. Kids sometimes play their own version of adult ball games, without the benefit of a court. They may also play with bows and arrows and spears.

You may see people playing a board game similar to checkers, called *bul*. Bul is lots of fun and not terribly hard, so don't be hesitant to join in if you're invited. Each side starts with five game pieces (seeds, beans, or something similar). Players toss a set of four flat corn kernels, each with a black spot burned into one side, as they would throw dice. The number of kernels that fall with the black mark up determines how many spaces the player can move a piece on the board. The object of the game is to capture an opponent's piece by landing on the same space. Players then drag that piece with them as they move back to their side of the board. The opponent's piece is then "dead" and out of the game,

A vase painting shows two Mayans playing a board game.

but the captor's piece can reenter. When a player has "killed" all the opponents, he or she has won the game.

FISHING

Fishing is more than just an enjoyable way to spend an afternoon—the locals fish for food. Fish are quite abundant in the area's rivers, freshwater lakes, and the sea. In larger waters, the locals use nets to catch the fish.

You may be astonished to see fishers standing near a dam, simply picking up fish that float to the surface as if by magic. The Maya place narcotic drugs from certain plants in the water above the dam. As the fish pass through the water and absorb the drugs, they pop to the surface in a stupor, making easy pickings for the locals.

TIME TO RELAX

After a day of sightseeing, nothing takes out the kinks like a relaxing steam bath. Public saunas are very common here and in many other parts of Mesoamerica. Located in buildings near the central plazas of most Mayan cities, saunas are popular with nobles, but adult visitors may use them, too. Bathers take off their clothes, sit on a stone bench and relax while servants pour water over hot rocks to create a bath of steam. Afterward, the bathers step into the next room to cool off. The locals use the steam baths to treat fevers, cramps, joint pain, and even poisonous bites and stings. You may see a servant using a bunch of herbs, dipped in water, to gently beat the problem area.

WHERE TO STAY

Ancient Mayan houses have thatched roofs, which keep out rain and allow heat to escape.

PUBLIC ACCOMMODATIONS

You won't find hotels or inns among the Maya. However, religious pilgrims willing to pay for food, offerings for the gods, and lodging often come to Mayan centers. In fact, the locals living near large religious centers, such as Tikal and Chichén Itzá, count on these travelers to earn a living, so you should be able to find a place to stay.

PRIVATE HOMES

Staying with one of the locals is the best way to experience the Mayan culture. Your host's home will probably be part of a complex of two to six dwellings built on a low dirt or rubble platform. All dwellings face a center courtyard, where most of the cooking and socializing takes place. Grandparents, married children, brothers and sisters, or other relatives may all live within this complex. Some of the buildings may be set aside as workshops, storage sheds, or kitchens. Others might be for servants' quarters.

The buildings are rectangular and have one or two rooms each. The Maya use stone or adobe blocks (a mixture of mud and straw or other binding material) for the walls. They use thatch (grass or straw) to create peaked roofs. The Maya don't have doors in their homes, but there may be a cloth or blanket hung across the entryway. The climate is mild, so this is all the protection you need.

If you stay in the home of one of the locals, they will probably offer you a bed that is really low to the ground. The bed frames are made from saplings and covered with a woven straw mat. Don't expect much privacy—the Maya all sleep in the same room. A screen or wall separates the sleeping quarters from the kitchen and living area.

Wooden stools and benches are about the only other big furniture you'll see in most homes. You will also see baskets, small wooden chests, cotton bags, pottery, and stone tools. Often the Maya hang bunches of chile peppers from the inside of the thatched roof. When the peppers dry out, cooks can reach up and pick one to season food. You may notice a hollowed out tree trunk outside the house. This is a bee pot, where bees make honey. Don't worry, though. The Maya raise a type of bee that has no stinger.

Chile peppers dry in the sun. The ancient Mayans use peppers to spice up their dishes.

WHAT TO EAT

MEALTIMES

If you like corn, you've come to the right place. Tortillas and tamales made from ground corn are the most common foods. An average man may eat nearly twenty tortillas at a single meal. The locals even make popcorn.

Tamales—ground corn wrapped in corn leaves and boiled in water—are popular. If the Maya offer you tortillas, use your fingers to dip the tortillas into the small dishes of condiments. Take care, though. The dishes can be hot! They often contain crushed chile peppers mixed with a little water and seasoned with salt. In one of the dishes you might find *buul,* or boiled black beans.

The common folk eat mainly corn, chiles, and beans (the poorest folks may even have trouble getting beans). Because of this diet, you should be warned that flatulence (passing gas) is quite common here.

COMMON FOODS

Although the local diet is centered around corn, you will find beans, squash, sweet potatoes, papayas, and pineapples, too. There are also several green leafy plants, which can be cooked like spinach. You will probably eat a lot of squash, which the locals usually boil. The hard outer shell of the squash is used to make bowls, serving utensils, and even babies' rattles.

(Facing page) *A mural in Bonampak shows nobles at a feast.*

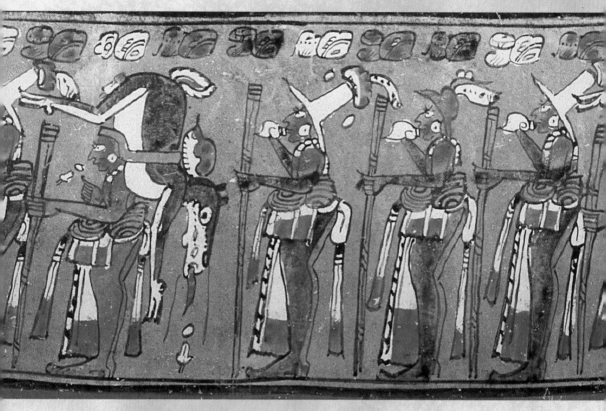

Carrying their blowguns (weapons) and two deer into their village, hunters blow into conch shells to announce their arrival.

The Maya hunt fox, peccary (wild pigs), raccoon, jaguar, armadillo, rabbit, opossum, coatimundi, tapir, monkey, porcupine, iguana, and squirrel for food. The lowland forest is also home to the paca, a large rodent. At the evening meal, expect a sort of stew made with vegetables, herbs, and whatever meat or fish might be available.

Hot Hint

If you come across the phrase "k'ik'bil," or "dog food," you should know that it does not refer to food for dogs. Here, dogs are food.

Fresh venison (deer meat) is highly valued, and a deer haunch is considered a good sacrifice for the gods. (It even has its own glyph.) A piece of dried venison served with balls of ground maize, wrapped in leaves and soaked in water flavored with chile peppers is a common lunch for farmers working in the fields.

Turkey and seafood are popular meals among the upper classes. Common folk eat such fare only on special occasions. Some locals keep flocks of tame turkeys and ducks, which are valued for their feathers as well as their meat. In some areas, the locals mix turkey with dog meat! The Maya also raise doves and curassows,

. . . the festival in the summer to celebrate the harvest. Don't be alarmed if girls throw popcorn at you—it's just part of the celebration. The girls then dance in a procession, rejoicing in a successful harvest.

Back TO THE Future

Discover the thick, milky liquid that oozes out of the wild sapodilla tree when it is cut. The locals let this stuff harden and then chew on it. Eureka! They've invented chewing gum. *Cha* (gum) is so important here that Kukulcan (the "Feathered Serpent" who is worshiped as a god) is a gum chewer. Although people living in the forests of Mexico will chew gum for centuries, it won't be discovered in the United States until 1870.

large birds similar to turkeys, for their meat. They eat bird eggs and iguana eggs, too.

If you are near a river or lake, you may eat jute (a type of snail) and fish such as mojarra and catfish. On the coast, you may get to try sea turtle, which is an important source of food for the locals. The locals also eat crab, shrimp, and lobster. It may shock you to see the locals dining on manatees. These large sea animals are in plentiful supply here and won't become endangered for more than one thousand years.

During your visit, you may see gardens with avocados, pawpaws, guavas, and soursops, all of which yield tasty fruits. Locals also grow melons and mulberries and eat wild fruits.

Don't be surprised if you come across some familiar tastes. The locals use honey to flavor food and drinks. You may also find vanilla, allspice, coriander, and oregano. If you like hot spicy food, you are in luck—chile pepper is a popular flavoring and an important part of the Mayan diet, providing essential vitamins and seasoning. In coastal areas, the salt that locals harvest from evaporated seawater is an important trade item.

Would You Care for a Beverage with That?

Most Maya do not eat much during the day, but they drink *posol,* a beverage made from boiled, crushed corn that has been dissolved in water. The locals seldom drink water by itself. If you are terribly thirsty and cannot find anything to drink, ask for a plant called *valapohov.* The locals chew on the moist leaves to quench their thirst.

By far the best beverage is chocolate, which the locals make by roasting cacao beans, grinding them, and mixing the ground beans with maize flour. Because cacao beans are so valuable, chocolate is expensive. Rich people can afford it. They even have special thermoslike pots in which to store the tasty beverage.

A censer, such as this
one made of pottery,
is used to hold sticks
of incense.

WHERE TO FIND SOUVENIRS

ARTS, CRAFTS, & OTHER DELIGHTS

Most major Mayan cities have central markets. The markets are only open on certain days of the week or during festivals, so you'll have to ask around to find out which days are market days. At the market, people come from other parts of Mesoamerica to buy, swap, get news, or just hang out.

Traders and merchants offer a variety of goods. You may see fans made from colorful feathers. Servants use them to brush flies away from their masters. Ceremonial shields, skirts, knee ornaments (decorative bands worn just below the knee), and bracelets will be for sale, too. Keep an eye out for wonderful headdresses made from paper-thin bark and brilliant feathers.

Jade jewelry is quite popular and easy to find. The locals cut the jade, carve it, and then polish it into beautiful earrings, bracelets, collars, and anklets. You may also see small jade statues. Jade bead necklaces make particularly nice gifts. The Maya also make jewelry from colorful shells, but these aren't nearly as valuable as jade jewelry.

BACK TO THE FUTURE

Mayan jade is actually jadeite, different from the common Chinese jade seen in modern times. Mayan jade is more uneven in color, less translucent, and slightly harder.

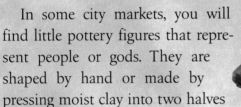

SIDE TRIP TRIVIA

You may have heard that the ocarina *(right)*, a small pottery flute, was invented in Europe in the 1800s. If you travel during the 800s or later, you will find the Maya are already making and playing ocarinas, some of which are shaped like humans or animals.

In some city markets, you will find little pottery figures that represent people or gods. They are shaped by hand or made by pressing moist clay into two halves of a clay mold and then pressing the pieces together before firing (baking at a high temperature to harden). The Maya often whitewash the figures—which are usually four to ten inches tall and made from a smooth, orange clay (the natural color of the clay in the area)—and then paint them. Examine these closely. They may be quite delicate with details such as facial tattoos and jeweled necklaces. Look for the ones that rattle or have a whistle built into the base.

Look for mosaics, which the locals make out of pieces of turquoise, jade, shell, and pyrite, a mineral that shines like metal. The Maya decorate pottery, masks, and even the sides of buildings with mosaic designs.

Musical instruments, such as the *pax*—a drum made from the shell of a small tortoise—make great souvenirs. The Maya usually carve and paint the shell with a lacquer (varnish) made from crushed insects. They also make trumpets from conch shells. Flutes are fashioned from baked clay, reeds, or bone. You may even see flutes made from human leg bones.

Another interesting item is a type of incense called copal, or pom. The Maya make pom from a local resin (sap). They form the resin into little cakes and paint the hardened cakes a pretty turquoise blue. When burned, pom gives off a fragrant odor.

If you expect to find gold masks, jewelry, or other gilded treasures here, you will be disappointed. There is no gold in the area. What little gold you may see has been brought from other areas through trade. The locals actually are unimpressed with gold. The Mayan word for gold, *takin*, means "excrement of the sun." In fact, you may see gold used for such ordinary objects as fishhooks!

Back TO THE FUTURE

Pay particular attention to Mayan wood carvings. Very few pieces will survive into modern times due to the damp Mayan climate. You may find masks, panels carved with scenes of everyday life, helmets, book covers, or other objects made from wood. Nearly all of these will be lost over the centuries to come.

How to Stay Safe & Healthy

A statuette of a grand priest. In ancient Mayan times, priests practice the art of healing in addition to their religious duties.

Take Two Woodpeckers' Bills & Call Me in the Morning

Some of the diseases you may encounter while visiting the Mayan civilization will be familiar. Pneumonia, rheumatism, epilepsy, indigestion, toothache, and cancer are common illnesses. The locals may also suffer from dysentery, stomach worms, and jaundice.

Now Hear This

A handy list of treatments compiled from local sources:

Toothache: Grate with a fishskin the tooth of a crocodile and let it be wrapped with cotton-wool . . . and applied to the tooth that throbs.

Sneezing: Take a handful of orange leaves, boil them, apply (the liquid) to the foot and then you rub the body with the liquid also.

Insanity: Take the testicles of a black cock, mash and dissolve them in cold water and give it to him to drink at dawn before he takes his breakfast. Every day at dawn he is to drink it.

If you become ill while traveling in the Mayan world, it's likely that the locals will think you are under the influence of an evil spirit. The key to good health and survival is to enlist the help of a priest or shaman (medicine man) to determine who or what is responsible for the illness. To do this, the shaman uses a variety of techniques. He may toss dice or bones, burn incense, or examine omens. Treatment usually involves a combination of prayer, ceremony, medicine, and sacrificial offerings.

The Maya rely on plants for medicine. One treatment you may recognize (but not as a treatment) is tobacco. The locals consider it somewhat of a cure-all. They also use the euphorbia plant, guavas, and sap from the rubber tree as medicines for diseases such as dysentery. Common Mayan medicines include fungi mixed with boiled tapir dung, a whole bat or live toad dissolved in a fermented drink, woodpeckers' bills, red worms, blood, crocodile testicles, bat wings, and bird fat. And you thought medicines at home tasted bad!

LOCAL DISEASES & DANGERS

You should be alert while walking in rain forests and swamps. Travelers can easily stumble upon wildlife that can be extremely dangerous. It's likely that you will encounter some deadly snakes, for example. Highly venomous coral snakes, rattlesnakes, water moccasins, and the fer-de-lance (a deadly type of pit viper), are just a few of the snakes that slither along Mayan ground. You could spot some scorpions, too. You will also find minor but annoying stinging and biting insects such as mosquitoes, gnats, fleas, ticks, chiggers, biting flies, and wasps.

The climate can be a source of trouble, too. In the tropical rain forest of the lowlands, humidity is so high that mold grows everywhere. Mold can cause lots of problems for people with allergies. The high humidity causes more unusual difficulties. If you are having trouble hearing, you may find that the problem is the growth of tiny mushrooms inside your ear!

DISASTERS, CATASTROPHES, & OTHER ANNOYANCES

Watch out for earthquakes and volcanoes in the southern part of the ancient Mayan civilization. This volcanic activity has produced some remarkable rocks, such as obsidian, that are so tough they can be used to cut through almost anything.

You may also encounter hurricanes in the fall. Caribbean hurricanes frequently hit the lowland areas without warning. These windy storms not only flood the trade routes that you will be traveling, but they destroy many crops, too, so food might be in short supply. On the bright side, the winds of a major hurricane can clear a field for cultivation by handily uprooting an entire forest.

(Facing page) *Mayan warriors battle with their enemies.*

WATCH FOR WARS

If you visit before the Spanish conquerors arrive in the early 1500s (which is highly recommended), you probably won't run into any wars. You should, however, be on the lookout for battles between neighboring groups.

Unpleasantness is increasingly common during the 700s and 800s. You may observe raids between neighboring groups, and this may upset your travel plans. In some cases, entire kingdoms may be shut down.

If you must visit during wartime, travel during the spring or summer, when farmers are busy in the fields. Farming takes priority over fighting. Battles are only fought during the dry season in the fall, when there aren't many farm tasks.

Because soldiers have to care for crops and transport all materials and supplies on foot, battles are usually close to home. Women go along as well, to prepare food for the troops. Fighting ends at sunset, so the men may eat their dinner.

The goal of Mayan battle is to take prisoners, gain prestige, and capture the enemy's standard—a flag believed to contain the opponent's power and spirit. In hand-to-hand combat, the victors overpower enemy warriors, strip them of their battle gear, and take them back to their city. The victors make slaves of low-ranking captives and sacrifice captives of high rank. The locals believe that sacrificing prisoners increases the prestige of the winning side's ruler and provides proper offerings to the gods. Capturing and sacrificing a neighboring ruler is the top achievement. When a ruler dies, the Maya believe the connection between the ruler's people and the gods is broken. Such a catastrophe greatly weakens the opponent's kingdom.

LAW & ORDER

Be sure to observe all rules and laws while you are visiting the Mayan civilization. The locals take law and order quite seriously. The Maya are particularly tough on people who commit crimes against their own family or neighbors, although this is quite rare.

"You break it, you bought it," is the law here. If you knock over someone's beehive, for example, you will be expected to pay for it—even if it was a mistake. The Maya don't believe in accidents, so people are expected to fix whatever wrongs they may cause.

The Maya consider stealing from neighbors to be disgraceful, so it doesn't happen much. If it does, the thief is expected to return or to pay for the stolen goods. If this is not possible, the thief has to work as a slave for the victim until the debt is paid. And that had better be the thief's last mistake. The locals have a "two strikes and you're out" law. A thief who steals a second time is put to death.

Tech Talk

In the 900s, the Maya invent a new type of armor. They soak quilted cotton tunics in a salt brine to stiffen the already dense fabric. This helps prevent arrows from piercing the warrior's flesh.

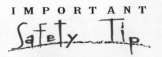

If you are responsible for someone else's death, you will be executed, even if the killing was an accident.

Take note that some things you might not think of as crimes are punished here. For example, because music and dance are important in religion, a musician who plays a wrong note or a dancer who loses the rhythm may be punished. A sculptor who makes a mistake in the representation of a god may also be punished.

Murder is punishable by death. According to Mayan beliefs, murderers are under the influence of an evil spirit. The only way to eliminate that evil spirit is to kill the person who harbors it.

Who's Who in the Ancient Mayan Civilization

Bird Jaguar

Bird Jaguar—a Mayan warrior and leader—was born in 709. He is the son of Shield Jaguar, who rules Yaxchilán when Bird Jaguar is born. (Shield Jaguar is worth meeting as well. He rules for more than sixty years and doesn't die until the year 742, when he is in his mid-nineties.) If you visit in 752, you may be able to take part in the ceremonies where Bird Jaguar becomes ruler of Yaxchilán. In the years leading up to 752, Bird Jaguar had some great military victories. In one he captured another Mayan lord, whose name glyph is a skull outlined by dots. This is why you may hear the locals refer to Bird Jaguar as Captor of Jeweled Skull.

Chan Muan

Chan Muan becomes ruler of Bonampak in about 776 after winning a great battle. The people of Bonampak honor him with a spectacular wall mural. In the mural, he is shown leading a jungle raid to capture victims for sacrifice and slavery. Chan Muan holds his enemy by the hair, a Mayan display of victory. Some Maya say that in real life, he wears the beaded skull of a defeated foe around his neck. If you visit between 790 and 792, you might be able to attend the ceremony in which Chan Muan's son is named heir to the throne, one of the most important rituals in Mayan culture.

PACAL

Pacal ("Shield") is easy to recognize. He is about six feet tall, nearly a foot taller than most of the locals. If you visit on July 29, 615, the day Pacal becomes ruler of Palenque, you can see him take over the throne from his mother, Lady Zac Kuk (Pacal is the twelve-year-old in the center of things). Under his long rule, Palenque becomes very powerful and rules a wide area. A forward-thinking kind of guy, Pacal orders the priests to calculate the date of the eightieth anniversary of the event—October 23, 4772! This date is carved on a tablet in the Temple of Inscriptions, one of Pacal's many construction projects. Pacal's tomb is so well hidden that archaeologists don't find it until the mid-1900s.

YAX PAC

Yax Pac ("Rising Sun") gains the throne in Copán in 763. If you visit after 773, you will find him at Sacred Mountain, his home and a place of ritual. Yax Pac is known for the dedication of an important temple, where at least fifteen jaguars are sacrificed and then buried. Historians think the jaguars may have represented the spirits of the fifteen rulers of Copán who came before Yax Pac.

LADY ZAC KUK

When Ac Kan, ruler of Palenque, dies in 612, the only heir to the throne (his younger brother, Pacal) is already dead. As a result, Pacal's daughter, Lady Zac Kuk, takes the throne. She rules for three years. Then her son, also named Pacal, takes over as ruler of Palenque. She is not the first female ruler, however. Her uncle, Ac Kan, had inherited the throne from his mother, Lady Kanal Ikal.

Preparing for the Trip

Play Bul

Archaeologists have discovered bul game boards scratched into the stone floors of Mayan buildings. Create your own bul board and play a game. You will need:

> 15 buttons, corn kernels, or chocolate chips
> 10 sticks or seeds for game pieces
> a pair of dice

1. On a flat surface, place 15 corn kernels in a row. Space them 2 inches apart. The spaces between the kernels will be the game board.
2. Each player gets 5 game pieces and one end of the board to call home.
3. Players begin the game by placing one of their pieces at the first space on their end of the board. Roll the dice to decide who goes first.
4. Each player rolls 1 die, moves his or her game piece, and then rolls and moves again to complete his or her turn. If a player should reach the end of the board, he or she begins again from the home space.
5. To win the game, a player must capture all of the opponent's pieces. If a player lands on a space occupied by the opponent, the opponent's piece is removed from the game. The captor sets his or her next game piece on the home space and proceeds with his or her turn.

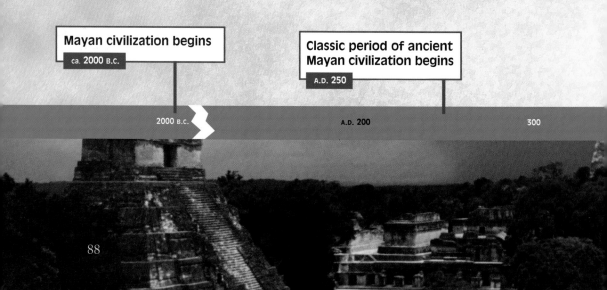

Mayan civilization begins	Classic period of ancient Mayan civilization begins
ca. 2000 B.C.	A.D. 250

2000 B.C.　　　　　　　　A.D. 200　　　　　　　　300

EAT LIKE THE MAYA

Before your trip, you might want to get used to the Mayan diet. Although Mayan tortillas are made with corn flour and this recipe uses wheat flour—an ingredient that's easier to find in modern times—the idea is the same. You might want to ask an adult for help. Enjoy!

1 cup flour	1 teaspoon salt
1/4 cup shortening	1/2 cup warm water

In a large bowl, combine the flour and the shortening. Use your fingers to work the flour into the shortening until it's broken down into lumps the size of peas. In a small bowl, combine the water and salt. Pour the water into the flour mixture. Work the water into the flour with your hands. Knead for ten minutes. Divide the dough into 1½-inch-diameter balls (about the size of golf balls). Place one ball on a flat, clean, surface. Sprinkle with flour. Use a rolling pin to roll each ball into a large, flat circle, about the size of a dinner plate. Stack the rolled-out tortillas on a plate, placing sheets of wax paper between each one. Heat a frying pan on medium high. Carefully place a tortilla in the center of the pan. Cook each side for twenty seconds. Use a pancake turner to flip the tortilla. Stack finished tortillas on a plate and cover to keep warm. Serve the tortillas with a thin layer of salsa on top.

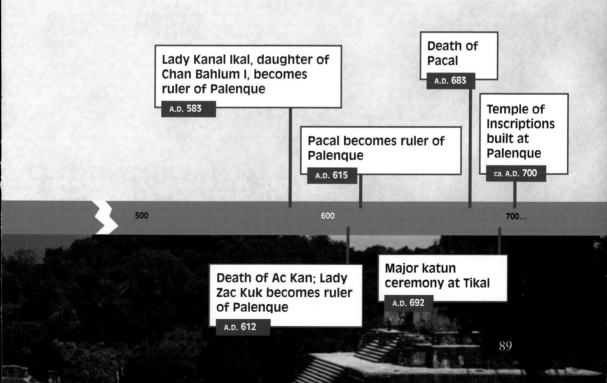

Lady Kanal Ikal, daughter of Chan Bahlum I, becomes ruler of Palenque
A.D. 583

Death of Pacal
A.D. 683

Temple of Inscriptions built at Palenque
ca. A.D. 700

Pacal becomes ruler of Palenque
A.D. 615

500   600   700...

Death of Ac Kan; Lady Zac Kuk becomes ruler of Palenque
A.D. 612

Major katun ceremony at Tikal
A.D. 692

89

GLOSSARY

astrology: the belief and study of the mystical or supernatural influence of the stars and planets on human life and activities

astronomy: the scientific study of stars, planets, and other celestial bodies

cacao: a South American evergreen tree that produces seeds known as cacao beans

cenote: a deep limestone well that occurs naturally

codex (pl. codices): an ancient manuscript or book. The Maya codices were usually written on paper made from tree bark and contained information about Mayan culture and daily life.

equinox: a day occurring twice a year when the Sun crosses the equator and there are equal hours of day and night

glyph: a symbolic figure or character representing a sound or a word. Each ancient Mayan glyph is a detailed picture with several parts.

Mesoamerica: a region inhabited by ancient civilizations, such as the Maya, that includes modern El Salvador, Honduras, Belize, Guatemala, and much of Mexico

mosaic: a picture or design made up of many small pieces of stone, shell, or other material

shaman: a priest or religious leader. The ancient Mayan shamans conducted ceremonies and were believed to be capable of contacting spirits and healing the sick.

Spanish Conquest: a period between the early and mid-1500s during which Spanish explorers and soldiers (also called conquistadors) arrived in Mesoamerica and conquered the Maya and other native peoples, claiming the land for Spain

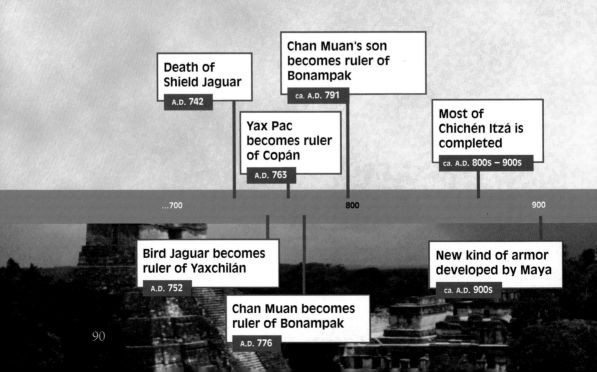

Death of Shield Jaguar
A.D. 742

Chan Muan's son becomes ruler of Bonampak
ca. A.D. 791

Yax Pac becomes ruler of Copán
A.D. 763

Most of Chichén Itzá is completed
ca. A.D. 800s – 900s

...700   800   900

Bird Jaguar becomes ruler of Yaxchilán
A.D. 752

New kind of armor developed by Maya
ca. A.D. 900s

Chan Muan becomes ruler of Bonampak
A.D. 776

Pronunciation Guide

cenote	seh-NOH-tay
Chichén Itzá	chee-CHEHN eet-SAH
ex	ESH
Itzamná	eets-ahm-NAH
Ix Chel	EESH CHEHL
katun	kah-TOON
Kukulcan	koo-kuhl-KAHN
k'ul ahau	KOOL ah-HOW
mano	MAH-noh
metate	meh-TAH-tay
nacom	nah-KOHM
Pacal	pah-KAHL
Palenque	pah-LEHN-kay
sacbeob	SAHK-bay-ahb or sahk-BAY-ahb
stelae	STEE-lee
Uaxactún	wah-shahk-TOON
uinal	oo-EE-nahl or WEE-nahl
Uxmal	oosh-MAHL
Yax Pac	YAHSH PAHK
Yucatán	yoo-kuh-TAHN
Lady Zac Kuk	ZAHK KOOK

Spanish Conquest of Maya; Bishop Diego de Landa records information about the Maya

ca. A.D. 1500s

Popol Vuh written

ca. A.D. 1550

1000   1500   1600

Christopher Columbus encounters the Maya

A.D. 1502

FURTHER READING

Books

Crosher, Judith. *Technology in the Time of the Maya.* Austin, TX: Raintree Steck-Vaughn Publishers, 1998.

Fisher, Leonard Everett. *The Gods and Goddesses of Ancient Maya.* New York: Holiday House Inc., 1999.

Greene, Jacqueline Dembar. *The Maya.* New York: Franklin Watts, 1992.

Linares, Frederico Navarrete. *A Maya.* Minneapolis: Runestone Press, 2000.

MacDonald, Fiona. *Step into the Aztec & Mayan Worlds.* Lorenz Books, 1998.

Schlesinger, Arthur Meier, ed. *Ancient Civilizations of the Aztecs and Maya: Chronicles from National Geographic.* New York: Chelsea House Publishers, 1999.

Stuart, Gene S., and George E. Stuart. *Lost Kingdoms of the Maya.* Washington, D.C.: National Geographic Society, 1993.

The World Heritage. *Mayan Civilization.* New York: Children's Press, 1993.

Internet Sites

Maya Adventure
<http://www.sci.mus.mn.us/sln/ma>

Maya Astronomy Page
<http://www.astro.uva.nl/~michielb/maya/astro.html>

The Mayan Temple
<http://www.ruf.rice.edu/~jchance/maya.html>

Rabbit in the Moon
<http://www.halfmoon.org>

BIBLIOGRAPHY

Bower, Bruce. "Sacred Secrets of the Caves." *Science News* (January 24, 1998): 56–58.

Burland, C. A. *The Ancient Maya*. New York: The John Day Company, 1967.

Carlson, John B. "America's Ancient Skywatchers." *National Geographic* (March 1990): 76–107.

Culbert, T. Patrick. *The Lost Civilization: The Story of the Classic Maya*. New York: Harper & Row Publishers, 1974.

Freidel, David, Linda Schele, and Joy Parker. *Maya Cosmos: Three Thousand Years on the Shaman's Path*. New York: William Morrow & Co., 1993.

Gallenkamp, Charles. *Maya: The Riddle and Rediscovery of a Lost Civilization*. New York: Viking, 1985.

Henderson, John S. *The World of the Ancient Maya*. Ithaca, NY: Cornell University Press, 1981.

James, Peter, and Nick Thorpe. *Ancient Inventions*. New York: Ballantine Books, 1994.

Miller, Mary. "Maya Masterpiece Revealed at Bonampak." *National Geographic* (February 1995): 50–69.

Morley, Sylvanus G., and George W. Brainerd. *The Ancient Maya*. Stanford, CA: Stanford University Press, 1983.

National Geographic World. "Time Travelers." *National Geographic World* (April 1991): 21–27.

Schele, Linda, and Mary Ellen Miller. *The Blood of Kings: Dynasty and Ritual in Maya Art*. New York: George Braziller, Inc., 1986.

Sharer, Robert J. *TheAncient Maya*. Stanford, CA: Stanford University Press, 1994.

Stuart, Gene S., and George E. Stuart. *Lost Kingdoms of the Maya*. Washington, D.C.: National Geographic Society, 1993.

Time-Life Books. *The Magnificent Maya*. Alexandria, VA: Time-Life Books, 1993.

Whitlock, Ralph. *Everyday Life of the Maya*. New York: G. P. Putnam's Sons, 1976.

Wolfgang von Hagen, Victor. *The Ancient Sun Kingdoms of the Americas*. Cleveland, OH: The World Publishing Company, 1961.

INDEX

ABOUT THE AUTHOR

Nancy Day is the author of nine books and forty-five articles for young people. She loves to read and is fascinated with the idea of time travel, which she says is "actually history in a great disguise." Her interest in time travel inspired the Passport to History series. Nancy Day lives with her husband, son, and two cats in a house that was built in 1827—before the Civil War. She often imagines what it would be like to go back in time to meet the shipbuilder who once lived there.

Acknowledgments for Quoted Material p. 8, as quoted by Robert J. Sharer, *The Ancient Maya* (Stanford, CA: Stanford University Press, 1994); p. 47, as quoted by Sylvanus G. Morley and George W. Brainerd, *The Ancient Maya* (Stanford, CA: Stanford University Press, 1983); p. 81, as quoted by Charles Gallenkamp, *Maya: The Riddle and Rediscovery of a Lost Civilization* (New York: Viking, 1985); p. 82, as quoted by Ralph Whitlock, *Everyday Life of the Maya* (New York: G. P. Putnam's Sons, 1976).

Photo Acknowledgments
The images in this book are used with the permission of: © Charles & Josette Lenars/Corbis, pp. 2, 61, 80; © Galen Rowell/Corbis, pp. 6–7; © Dallas and John Heaton/Corbis, pp. 10–11; © M. Bryan Ginsberg, pp. 12–13; © Tom Boyden, p. 14; © Jack Fields/Corbis, p. 17; © D. Donne Bryant/DDB Stock Photography, pp. 18, 30, 43, 54, 55; © Enzo & Paolo Ragazzini/Corbis, pp. 20, 88–89, 90–91; © Danny Lehman/Corbis, p. 23; © Craig Lovell/Corbis, p. 25; © D. Donne Bryant/Art Resource, NY, p. 26; © Hans Georg Roth/Corbis, p. 28; © Owen Franken/Corbis, p. 31; © Justin Kerr, pp. 32–33, 38, 44–45, 62, 64–65, 72–73; Antochiw Collection/The Art Archive, pp. 34, 68; Independent Picture Service, p. 37; © Paul Meyers, p. 40; Werner Forman/Art Resource, NY, pp. 42, 57; The Granger Collection, pp. 46, 48, 66; © Erich Lessing/Art Resource, NY, p. 49; SEF/Art Resource, NY, p. 50; © Gianni Dagli Orti/Corbis, pp. 52, 70, 76, 78, 83; Archeological Museum Mexico/The Art Archive, p. 53; Art Resource, NY, p. 56; © Macduff Everton/Corbis, p. 59; © Robert Holmes/Corbis, p. 69; © Danielle Gustafson/Art Resource, NY, p. 86; Scala/Art Resource, NY, p. 87.

Front cover: Werner Forman/Art Resource, NY (upper left), © Erich Lessing/Art Resource, NY (bottom right).

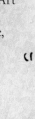